VINTAGE 2000

Vintage 2000 is an anthology of the best poems from the 2000 National Poetry Contest and the Canadian Youth Poetry Competiton.

The National Poetry Contest
2000 Prize Winners

FIRST PRIZE: Russell Thornton
"The Beginnings of Stars"

SECOND PRIZE: Sue MacLeod
"Especially for a woman, reading"

THIRD PRIZE: Tammy Armstrong
"A Proper Burial for Songbirds"

The Canadian Youth Poetry Competition
2000 Prize Winners

Senior Division

FIRST PRIZE: Sharon Page
"Water Buffalo + Emily = Love"

SECOND PRIZE: Mike Mulley
"The Deluge"

THIRD PRIZE: Robin Daniels
"Tea at High Acre, When I was a Boy"

Junior Division

FIRST PRIZE: Michael Coren
"The Graveyard"

SECOND PRIZE: Katie English
"There Upon a Lumpy Rock"

THIRD PRIZE: Jennifer Patterson
"Troubled Boys"

VINTAGE 2000

poems from

The National
Poetry Contest

&

The Canadian Youth
Poetry Competition

THE LEAGUE
of CANADIAN
POETS

RONSDALE PRESS

2000

RONSDALE PRESS
3350 West 21st Avenue
Vancouver, B.C., Canada
V6S 1G7

Set in New Baskerville: 10.5 pt on 13.5
Typesetting: Julie Cochrane
Printing: Hignell Printing, Winnipeg, Manitoba
Cover Art: Joe Plaskett, detail of *Abstract Improvisation,*
    1946, Watercolour, 18" x 12"
Cover Design: Julie Cochrane

Ronsdale Press wishes to thank the Canada Council for the Arts, the Government of Canada through the Book Publishing Industry Development Program (BPIDP), and the Province of British Columbia through the British Columbia Arts Council for their support of its publishing program.

ISBN: 0-921870-75-2

CANADIAN CATALOGUING IN PUBLICATION DATA

Main entry under title:

Vintage

    Annual.
    ISSN 1204-4504

    1. Canadian poetry (English) — 20th century.* I. League of Canadian Poets.
PS8279.V55   C811'.5408'005   C96-300232-5
PR9195.25.V55

Contents

Foreword

Each year the League of Canadian Poets sponsors the National Poetry Competition and the Youth Poetry Competition. Both have as their aim the encouragement of poetic talent.

The National Poetry Competion has been an annual event ever since its beginning in 1986 and is now one of Canada's most prestigious writing competitions, offering all Canadians a chance to discover their writing abilities. Six well known poets are selected by the League's National Council to judge the contest. The judgement criterion is straight forward: quality of writing. Each year the 50 winning poems of the National Poetry Contest are gathered into the poetry anthology *Vintage*. From these poems, the top three are chosen and cash prizes of $1,000, $750 and $500 are awarded.

The Canadian Youth Poetry Competition comprises two categories: the junior division for students in grades 7 to 9, and the senior division for grades 10 to 12 (OAC in Ontario). The judges are established poets who choose the top three poems in each category, with cash prizes of $500, $300 and $250 for each category. There are also a number of honourable mentions. The three prize poems in each category are included in *Vintage*.

Vintage 2000, published by Ronsdale Press, is available at book stores across Canada and also directly from the League of Canadian Poets. With poets represented from all over Canada and all age groups, *Vintage 2000* represents a broad range of writing styles and topics and offers an ideal introduction to the vitality and diversity of Canadian poetry.

The National
Poetry Contest

Introduction to the National Poetry Contest

Judges: Judith Krause, Dave Margoshes, Paul Wilson, Anne Campbell

There was this year, in the spring of 2000, in the province of Saskatchewan, a writers conference. At the conference a panel discussion was held; it was titled *The Currency of Poetry*. Several perspectives and definitions were presented including the Webster definition of currency: "a continual passing from hand to hand." But it was the definition of currency as exchange that animated the energetic discussion.

For me, what emerged was the question: *what it is that is being exchanged* when poetry is *working* at its best? By poetry I mean not simply verse, or social criticism or emoting, but language speaking in the present and across time, precisely, to our shared but diverse existence here on earth, speaking to our mutuality in a world in a continual process of becoming.

If poetry is language *moved* across time, to each of us, what is it that occurs within us, as readers, when that language or *working poetry* is received?

For me, the something that occurs is exchange. Working poetry received *liberates* some part of my being. At a deep level some resting, or sleeping, or perhaps waiting part of my mind/body/being is touched, brought alive or awakened, confirmed, quickened or enlivened. This through the specificity of the (poetry) language spoken, and received. Poetry has purchased some part of my being, brought it to light and placed it in my world, for choice. Poetry has been received and, in exchange, some part of me is free, or present in the world in a new way.

This act, the act of poetry working in such a way, is a gift of such amazement that it is almost never completely achieved. When we are touched by the words of those who do achieve or come very close to it we are (often) speechless with the *knowing* that has occurred. We are grateful for poems that are this complete and, equally important, we are grateful for those sections, lines, or even words, within a poem that in themselves are complete.

So it is with the poems selected here: the best poems explore and animate the sensibility and/or mystery at their core, e.g., Russell Thornton's "The Beginnings of Stars"; or a poem contains a stanza so complete in itself it merits recognition: Julia McCarthy's "House of Feathers", the last stanza, "I still dream. . . ." Or a poem allows the experience of "Spotter", Terence Young's poem that catches our breath in recognition, and in the delight of a perfect line, ". . . It occurs to you that every moment you are alive / is an exercise in trust."

No question, writing schools, writing groups, regions, individual sensibilities and the diversity of interests amongst writers — all of these create a wide variety of views and tastes in poetry. But for me, all writers who enter competitions, as well as those whose work is chosen for publication, are to be congratulated. As a matter of fact, I am grateful for the impulse that evokes the hard work of poem-making by anyone.

We know an alternative jury might have made other selections. In competitions, jury members can each only honestly choose as they experience poems coming close to the work of poetry: for me, that is language used so well it animates and liberates from the dark, our very being.

— Anne Campbell
May 21, 2000

The National Poetry Contest
2000 Prize Winners

Russell Thornton
"The Beginnings of Stars"

Sue MacLeod
"Especially for a woman, reading"

Tammy Armstrong
"A Proper Burial for Songbirds"

The Beginnings of Stars

The late sun burning close, and slow waves coming in —
the sea's mysterious lit wine of touch
on the sand, slipping away glittering
in scattered glasslike grains for an instant,
and returning again; if we belong
to each other, we belong to that touch.
Then suddenly the sun is gone; the sky
is a dark purple darkening to black.
Those sky deities appear, those bright ones
inexorably performing their fixed
and millennia-old roles said to rule a life —
glints, coruscations, crushed glare-origins
within abundant rich clusters of grapes
spreading throughout the night's summer vineyard.
There are the never-beheld-before stars,
we wish we could say rightly and at last,
when we know even the closest we see
had to have been born more than long ago,
and the farthest born and died before that.
But since the light is the way we see light,
it must be travelling in a heaven
of more than our memory will allow,
where we ourselves might see how no person
or thing or love is ever gone, but visible,
and forever new, in light, and in us,
where light is always turning, flower-like,
opening and closing and opening.
We build a fire which will repeat at night
what the sun did during the day; the sparks
fly off and disappear the way the stars
will seem to disappear tomorrow in the sun.
The body is the wine-flask and the wine;
the lover is the veil on the beloved's face.

And what we hide within, and hides from us
through all our hours of light, seems dark, and yet,
now in the dark as in the one centre
of the fusions that are stars, is pure time,
when the bodies we are wake in their day,
and we taste that day's wine, that endless beginning
of nameless fate, when we give ourselves up
to our lives, and enter another life.

Especially for a woman, reading

Especially in the afternoon when light slants
through the window, grazing her cheek on its way to the page.
For a woman who appreciates that kind of light
for reading. Especially in mornings, when coffee makers
groan. When everyone else is still climbing, still hand-
over-handing their way
up from dreams. For the book
that fell into the bath
and was fished out — *quickly*. For the line
that swam before her as she fell
asleep. In stolen time: the check-out line, the way to work.
In fits and starts of traffic, in the press
of bodies. Especially
for anyone who's ever missed
her stop. For anyone who's laughed out loud while reading
in a restaurant. Or ever thought of writing
to a stranger:
You told my story. How did you know?

Especially for a teenage girl whose touch
turns bookmarks into ash. And so
she uses rubber bands, a roll of tape, a stray sock, a receipt,
    or *my* book
to hold *her* place open. Who won't
come to supper till she finishes her page.
For a grandmother I know
about, who stirred with a book in one hand. For everyone stirring
with words in their hands. For anyone who's ever grasped
a book in two hands.
Hold your breath, and crack it open.
For books that have burned to be written. Books
thrown into the fire
because supper wasn't ready, or her chores had not been done.

For anyone who's ever had anyone
tell her:
All that reading makes you think too much.

Especially when the leaves against the window
are a chorus from another time.
When evening comes, a woman stretches one curved arm to reach
the light behind her. She is reading
while the birds take roost, and punctuate
the branches. Reading till her book is finished. Reading
like a girl.

A Proper Burial for Songbirds

I Partita

Boreal winds through Howe Sound
edge the birds away from the island.
This morning belongs to them:
the last survivors who forget there is solidity
in the earth beneath their flight
who fall and glide like too many laundry tickets
from dresses I've forgotten who removed
at the end of an evening.

Autumn is housepaint, thick with rain.
Soon, they say in the cove, soon the rains will come,
in November when the songbirds go,
when the broken necked, the bruised axillae
are washed down past the property lines,
buried beneath buck-trodden mulch.

Pincette mouthed, their songs have pushed out
past early morning, hole-punching the mist
still hanging over Valhalla.
This charm of finches stripped the lilac bush of beetles,
sat high on the scattering of car parts the neighbour collects.
They are halation,
the sparks and embers from our unattended bonfires
stretched toward the skewer of lowtide,
the sparks that settled over damp beach stones,
glowing, breathing quickly as I have beneath your hands
in those plumb mornings before the birds woke
and began their songs again.

II Aubade

The kitten brings dead goldfinch to my desk —
weasel-bodied magus has no need
for these tokens of praise.
I leave it near the dictionaries and recipe cards,
wait until the sun slips through the pines,
lamella rays through the backyard,
through this hutch of a house I call home:
the hinge-stiff door, stained coffee mugs,
the rhubarb stalks, always mealy before picking.
The cats will not taste again,
they lose interest as I have with too much.

This Sunday morning, late summer.
Sunday not for burials but for cricket wheeze,
a lawn chair, chain saw whine some miles away.
We have lost the cadence between us,
I no longer remember where your significant scars lead,
light cigarettes too slowly this morning
and the room burns with singed tobacco.
It won't wake you.
The birdfeeder was blown down last night —
the squeak and pull on clothesline — a grace note
while songbirds in gypsy brights peck over our blighted lawn,
over the gold leaf rings where the rattans stayed all summer,
softening then splintering under the afternoon suns.

A dead finch
pale as the anemic yard trees,
skull feathers nearly the colour of infection,
I slide it outside on old newsprint
watch as it falls unapologetically
on the rusted fronds of last year's wood ferns.

Hands of the Father

One hundred thousand hours of paper,
printer's ink and pencilled estimates
have shaped his hands,
fingers sturdy as walking sticks.
On weekends they became instruments
for tying knots he could not name:
a clove-hitch supported the fences
when pasture thinned and cattle
stretched the page-wire; a bowline
steadied the TV antenna in gusts
that crossed the field; twin cat's paws
pulled his car doors together.

Their ancestry lies
in the hands of his father,
a merchant seaman who lies
in Bermuda, the charitable dairyman
of the great depression,
a bankrupt who left for sea
when his son was eight years old, whose hands
are a memory from a photograph.

To secure a calf for branding,
my father tied a random knot
of endless loops and bends,
a mystery neither sailor
nor mathematician could unravel.
This was his knot of knots:
a victory for the hands of the father

who holds his shining
radiated head, right hand
stroking his scalp for warmth, left hand
releasing comforting drops
until he says he has to go.

Sixty-four years of heat
dissipate through his hands.
They are laid to rest in his lap.

Letters to an agoraphobic mother from her claustrophobic daughter

#8

letters are maps
sections of days traveled
a flat topography
only a school girl faith in Columbus
sustains our belief that
the world is round

it is impossible to defy borders without stepping off the edge

we are map-makers
over eight years
between us
we have
974 blocks of cement
20 minutes of unused telephone wire
432 mailboxes
and too many doors

we run parallel
there are no intersections
where we meet
to construct a legend around
the excited flutter of hands in speech
that raises paper to clouds
as we sigh over the possibilities of flower gardens

language dries on the page
like a sun shower on pavement
an impotent sprinkling
it's the thunder we miss
an unreproducible voice
that echoes the roll of moments passing

we remain on the map. we live between the periods.
omitted are the names of side streets
the avenues that lead to the heart
of where we are

I can't explain
how knocking my head
against the jewelry store window glass
was funny

but for the cost of a stamp
the post office will carry fragments
in a canvas bag
and drop them
at our doors

we unfold the pages
iron them with our palms
creases run horizontal and vertical
like lines of latitude and longitude

love is always measured in degrees

A Collection of Stones

A collection of stones, each one blue-gray
from the belly of the world's white,
each lasting memory wrapped in
silken cloths and the gathering
of the red dust I kept.

What tracks I've laid down,
fade with purpose,
but I see the colourful collection
of cobblestones from Montreal
and the gumbo-coloured rocks from Regina;
and the body waits for more,
the hands turning every nugget
toward the light and the dark root's ruby
in my eyes as I'd lean and thrust my hand
into the quickening silt.

Something like crystals could spill before my anxious fingers,
the stones thrown and skipped across the beyond,
across the lake that deeply knows the strength of my arm
and the green quartz that shone when I was young.

How I ripped the mounds of dirt apart with my hands,
the fitful tearing and my fingers' plunge,
hoping the clots would produce just one gem;
through memory I chased the drifting dirt
and shifting sands, and the bucket
I attached to my hip, clanked, clanked again,
bruised me so I woke the next morning with
something like a shiner, my legs aching terribly,
and the settling dust of my caked-up eyes.

Long ago I followed the moistened shimmer,
the onyx wet and the geode's broken eggs,
the flicker of the crystal's terminations
and the blue-glass faces of the broken cliffs;
the narrow tumbling of the stone's retreat,
down it plunged, down, down, never
knowing how I waited to snatch
the crumbling prizes from the avalanche
and the pile I sifted through with glee.

When the night air became deep and azure
I went to the pond's calling, waited there,
dove headlong into the deepening shadows,
dredged up something like an emerald with perfect shine;
how it turned in my hand, sharp-edged, tiny little daggers
like the jaw of a cat, and the multifaceted glimmer that produced
my reflection.

Transplant

Michael is cleaning out the weeds
on the front lawn; I'm shocked
by how many of them I mistook for plants.
My landlord's feeling good these days, anxious
to clean house while he's up to it. Less excited
about going back to work
at the funeral home. He wears a falling-apart
t-shirt and sweats, he tears
at the unaccountable weeds in the yard,
yanking with his whole body. Pulling up roots,
attachments, the moisture-suckers, he tells me about his friend,
also with HIV,
who sits about all day,
refusing to do anything,
feeling, well — sorry.
The friend, he believes, is abusing the system.
He's *one of those*. As Michael says this,
he leans with all his weight,
loosening the rope-like vines
that have nowhere else to go,
that have entered the earth
and will not leave.

Vocabulary of a Bush Pilot's Wife

More often than not, I forget
that there were times my mother loved him —
and that she wasn't reserved
about it, that she was opened,

that she wasn't frail. That every gesture
was performed with certainty:
the abandoned job, the tongue stuck out
in defiance. But now she can say it —

We were still very much in love;
and I know this is what let her sleep
nights in small-town Quebec,
no company during the days
but the gas stove, the dictionary, the half-
done tapestry of a woman

sitting by the window, her long hair
in a loose, thick braid.

The Wedding Photograph Over Our Bed

In half-light, I see the photograph
in the mirror, white dress and hat
encasing the shadows of your face,

me nearly invisible in black suit,
a wing of white collar at my throat,
a retrospective flutter in my heart.

Each of our heads leans to each
as if teased by an urge to touch,
faces bronze like candlelit coins.

By light's sorcery we change sides.
I transpose left. You move right.
Our clasped hands reverse grips.

We've learned to make this trade
seem easy, our complex science
defying space to take the other's place.

Body Song To Hypnos

for Bill Hayes

Body knows what it wants,
roams through rooms frazzled,
rejects TV, snacks, books.

No pill-made phony doze
with vain shallow wipeout
and day-long after-grog.

Body wants what it knows
it hasn't had for years —
one real dream-laced sleep.

He studies the ways the cats
laze through seven-hour days
and snooze in languid ease.

Body yawns in envy at subway
dozers burrowed in sweaters,
their drooling mouths agog.

Hypnos in your Lemnos cave,
god of sleep, son-maker, sun-
taker, son of night, heed

as Body hums your hymns.
Sleep fixer, sweet warrior,
anoint him with your elixir.

Last Stand in Cottage Country

It begins with a tent puffed up
Against the winds the lake sends through.
Soon there's a shanty large enough
To change into bathing suits, sleep on cots
Lined up for the escaped suburban sardines
All having the same dream about running water
That wakes them each to crack open
A door between one darkness and another
Darkness with crickets playing bars between waves.

Soon there's a cabin — with windows large enough,
The kids are told, to be as good as TV.
Two years later there's a power line
And the fireplace is the coldest thing
In the place all summer. One year more
And a phone roosters them up with news
They cannot simply read from this morning's horizon.
Friends come for barbecues and clandestine shelling
Of muscles from shucked bathing suits.

There are, of course, other cottages and one day
One of them raises a flag. Another responds
With a rock garden. A volley of cannonballers
Sounds from a new dock. Sailboats and seadoos
Vie for command of these low seas. An A-frame chalet
Appears like an invasion of superior culture.
Its neighbour retaliates by putting in a basement
And a third floor with deck lording
Over the diminished triangular.

Boundary disputes intensify. Squabbles over who
Will pay what for repairs to the only road in or out.
How often someone may use another's well until
They drill for a substitute. They gossip
About the first dilapidated cabin, say
It's driving their property values down.
Couples begin to retire here with their silver plates
And satellite dishes. No one can recall
What was a party line.

I stood for a long while this morning on the shore,
Balancing on the edges of land and lake, unable
To remember from which way I had come.
I like to swim unseen in the middle of the lake
They all can't admit they share. The water builds
Wave after wave above me, getting it right
Effortlessly. I touch bottom but always have to
Come back up. Nothing down there will ever
Have my name. All I have is the thrill of trespassing
On the restless mind of the lake that everyone else
Toes with a chatter before turning back
To the thin path they've taken through
The crouching thorns. When I surface I see
All of them, the cottages in a semi-circle as if
Spiralling toward the lake. Cottagers listen
At night to the waves whispering over rock and sand.
They don't like what they pretend they can't hear —
Water calling to its half-brother, man.

Fog

This morning I felt the fog
before I saw its white rolling descent
hanging itself like gauze over the arbutus

and causing what is close to be
unattainable. For one moment I believed
I smelled eucalyptus, my feet

dusted with fine motes of sand.
I must have journeyed in the night.
Returned to seaside villages

where light is compromised
by particles of water, although the mist
has a certain density I can trust,

a weight, or substance one can gauge
relative to wind. A dampness capable
of penetrating clothing, skin, sometimes

loneliness. I woke this morning
to the absence of foghorns, unable to sustain
even the most inadvertent holiness.

Deception

You are brought to the details in spite of yourself. It is late January and in your backyard the Japonica tree, seduced by the warm breath of El Niño, pushes through dormant days to break open into winter. The buds falling hard and black on frozen ground.

There is that moment when you know you are only a host; that your blindness changes nothing.

This morning your fingers, moving casually over your breast, pause at the nub sprouting beneath your left nipple.

In the mirror your naked body familiar, and you startled, as if absent for years, somebody has finally called you home.

One year ago, after surgery, your friend showed you how she could move her arm. Raising it over her head, she looked at you like a child; a seven-year-old who has just learned to spell *porcelain*.

You are learning there is no way to circumvent the cold, the saplings snapping under their aureole of ice.

That Bright Singing

It was you who taught me about spirits.
Stretched out in the grass, our backs
against the cool ground, you spoke of your brother —
how the river held him like a secret
through the slow days of summer,
the sun glinting off the train bridge above us

breaking late afternoon into pieces, and us
with it. You were a boy fastened onto by spirits,
the lost ones who played alone, summer
after summer, the ones who stayed back
unable to leave, as if their death was a secret
kept from them. The way brothers

keep things from each other; a kind of brother-
hood of silence, swearing: *nothing can hurt us,*
believing both of you invincible. It was no secret
Ben was wild; crazy and high-spirited,
stealing the old man's hooch behind his back
drinking Calona Red that summer

yelling *Geronimo* into the wide open summer
sky, high on the silver bridge, your brother
followed his voice as it broke through the river's back
close to where we lie now, as if the current might show us
something new, something we had missed; as if his spirit
could break the silence, bending close, whisper his secrets.

What would he tell us of water? How salmon hide in secret
pools beyond the tip of your gaff pole each summer,
deep within filtered light their spirits
swimming, shadows on the riverbed, brothers
and sisters side by side. What would he ask of us?
A carving knife, a bottle of sweet wine? Would we back

away, startled to come so close, wish him back
to his dark green grave, or hold him like a secret,
move slightly to let him sleep between us
his dark hair floating on the pillow. Summer
again and the boys gather at the bridge, your brother
too. Watch as they fall, that bright singing, those spirits.

I dream of summer and the three of us
baking salmon on hot rocks, throwing bones and secrets back,
feeding the spirit of your crazy, hungry brother.

The Doctor's Wife

Each weekday my dark-suited father drove away,
white coat waiting in an office
much like the one my mother had left in Scotland.
Here, she sewed blue curtains for his windows
with her old Singer, long lines of stitches
like sutures she used to sew on women's bellies.

At dinner, she carved our roasts along the bone
with scalpel precision. She asked about his patients,
the doctors down the hall, remembered
when she wasn't a wife. He let her
give us shots at home for measles.
When we were sick, they argued.

Every month she waited for signs of a son inside her.
One almost came,
but changed its mind, gone
after a midnight rush to the hospital.

Then, in the fall when we left for school,
she dug a circle of soil, round as the moon,
in the expanse of yellowed lawn,
and planted a young rhododendron bush.

She watered and watched it through the winter.
Each leaf that grew or fell she counted.
My father scoffed, his practice blooming.
She'd wait by the window, arms crossed,
braced to shout at the boys who cut
across the right angles of our lawn.

After church one Sunday, she saw it first.
In the circle, churned earth,
a pile of twigs, the trunk jutting out
like a shard of bone.
She crouched beside it silently,
fingered each broken joint.

Learning Chinese

After English school, we took the bus three days a week
to a Chinese church basement and a teacher
who looked like Chairman Mao with a perm.

Dreaming of tv, we sat at tables
with our beige textbooks open to rhymes
about cows and sheep going up or down mountains,
and the shepherds who looked for them,
about good students who arrived early to school
while mothers made meals and fathers worked.

Each lesson, the teacher conducted
our choir of fingers, new words
poked, brushed and sliced into the air —
the three drops of water,
flat lines like rungs on a ladder,
lines straight down with slight flicks to the left,
or tapered tails, swooped in or out.

We learned how a mouth is a square
with a hollow inside, how two trees make a forest,
how the sun and the moon side by side
can be as bright as a mind, that peace
is a woman under the roof of a home,
how man stands in the centre,
of both fire and sky.

How I'll Make Love To You

I

a bare hotel room in South East Asia:
our balcony doors open like a widened eye
the sound of slaughter-bound chickens, angry
barter in the street below, automatic
gunfire from the hills, facing

each other on our sides, my leg
hooked over the small rise of your trousered hips,
the hem of my cotton dress lifted into the cradle
of my waist, your shirt still on, but open, the crispness
of your clothed leg against my skin:

silent, unmoving

    so

the brown boy on the balcony across the street thinks
we're just sleeping, does not see our eyes open
our skin joined in that foreign country
smaller than the palm of a child's hand

II

on the wool rug of your library:
the afternoon sun of winter falling
from a window above, warm
in the oldest way, I

on my stomach, naked as an empty scrapbook
Homer and Virgil stacked pillows beneath my cheek
you, with a glue stick tearing out pages of
Chekhov and Carver, Ginsberg and Hughes

pasting their words down my back, my legs,
covering my stomach, *Metamorphoses,*
crossing my breasts, *On the Road,*
Updike for shoes, paper wings from Marquez

you reach for your glasses
consume me slowly
word by word, beginning to end

III

in a restaurant lounge:
drunk on martinis and clams,
you sink back into pillows, anticipate
dessert, cigars and John Coltrane

my head shaved, my suit pressed
and you in wrinkled perfection, every hair askew
giddy with the feel of velvet upholstery
a promise of gluttony and excess, plastic
to pay the three-figure bill

stranded in the guilty bliss of let's pretend
refugees squatting in a five-star hotel

my hand between your legs as you order
crème brûlée and tell the waiter
to send the lobster back.

New Year's Eve

And I am reminded how much I hate being alone in the house at night, nothing in the background but the furnace kicking in and out, stirring up dust like an old bull, phone ringing frequently, never for me. Always I'm a little girl at this hour, watching the door, listening for the stranger's big boots. You're working a concert, our son sitting a baby girl, daughter at her first New Year's Eve party. Before she left, I reminded Taylor she's only twelve. What was trapped on her face suggested two possibilities. *Mom, what could you be imagining?* That's what she wanted me to see, but beneath that (I know, I've worn the look, too): *Mother, how could you know?*

New Year's Eve, and I'm alone with John Irving and all his writers in *A Widow For One Year.* I am ill, but not too ill to close this book, or dream I am a writer with a house in the Hamptons. If I were stronger, I'd kick off the blankets, find an atlas and see where the Hamptons are.

Our friend, the chiropractor, calls from Montana. His phone voice is something to be sipped slowly, but I don't say this. He's up with his baby, waiting for his wife, a nurse, to come home. Two days ago I was thinking of him, how proud I am of the shape his life has taken. We knew him before. At his thirtieth birthday party, he performed a striptease. There were black balloons, and I licked ouzo off some guy's chest. Most of the women in that house had loved him. We were all good friends. I want to tell him how I am happy for him. It has been a long time coming, his life, to where it is now, but I don't say it. I say nothing like this.

The wind's blowing another five inches of snow across the city. I look out the window and the white stings my eyes. Too late for Christmas, this snow. We no longer need it. Is there snow in the Hamptons? I examine the book, the bio notes. John Irving, a good-looking man, in jeans and a T-shirt. I like his thick hair, his leather (I'm guessing) office chair. He lives in Toronto and southern Vermont. A man who divides his time. I would like to be someone who divides my time between residences, not just responsibilities.

Another year turning like a page; I should feel something. I should mark it. But how? I've given up smoking and the better part of booze. I'm down to chocolate and there's none in the house.

The black dog slinks from room to room. He doesn't know it's the eve of his birthday, but he knows something's not right. There've been no runs for days, not one single car ride to appease him. So he slinks.

There are ninety minutes left of the year. I cross the kitchen floor like a patient, like a survivor of recent surgery. Diet Coke in a wine glass. So this is lonely.

I raise my glass to the birthday dog, a century folding, friends in far places, every good thing waiting in the next millennium, that soft white blanket of necessary faith we gather around our souls.

At The Lake

for Lorenka

The last strawberry daiquiri's downed, fire's
crackled out, the moon a drop of butterscotch
slung low across the lake. Already someone's
passed out or into that meditative state eased on
by alcohol and the easy comfort of old friends
who'll speak to you tomorrow, anyway. The youngest
children have run themselves out, the others,
swinging their legs over the edge of everything,
find what they need in the sand beyond your seeing.
There is only what's left of you — two women,
three men — all a little in love with each other.
You are playing darts. Your friend holds one hand
over her left eye: a skin patch, to slow the world
down. A moth lands on the board. The sun
is rising. You'll pay for this night later.
Now nothing's more important than nailing
the moth. The moth becomes the moment.
All through what's left of the night
everyone misses. Your laughter is summer,
birch bark and wings.

You tell me this story in Lloydminster.
It's been years, and we're well down the highway
to becoming our mothers. I've made the night
with the moths my own. This is who I've become.
Forgive me for rearranging nouns and the moon.
I was not there. I'm happy for the lake
in your life, the daiquiris and the man you love

who makes them. It may be too many years again
before our lives cross, even briefly, like tonight,
a meal together in this hotel. Time is a maze
we lose ourselves in. Thank you for meeting me.
Over the candles I was thinking what girls
we made on horses. I was listening. This matters.
I was trying to get it right.

Sunburst

Today, in a public washroom, a woman
reminded me of you, eerily, the twinned ghost to memory,
absently combing her hair and smiling, I could barely look away.
You are gone, we haven't spoken in years,
I'm twice as old as when we were seventeen,
driving a borrowed Camaro beneath Niagara street lights.

At twelve, we imagined ourselves champions on 10-speeds,
we played soccer, high school basketball and eventually, guitars;
you put me at ease, the first person I'd ever jammed with,
your heavy strum over rough Country & Western twang
against my flat-picked originals à la Joni and Neil. *Lotsa laughs.*
Remember when I worked at canoe camp — you sent that tape of you
covering Eagles' songs I wish I'd kept,
not letting my dislike for *Hotel California* get the better of me.

Eight winters ago my mom sent the home-town version of your story;
a wild statistic smudged on newsprint. Shocked by your
mortality, I was unable to articulate:
how to rappel the locked cells of memory,
illuminate any penetrable frill of the brain. We
lost contact. You
were murdered.
That blond man with a gun is still a fugitive.

Last week a woman on radio was describing the North in Canadian
     experience,
how people head there to escape, to discover
their bearings beneath an endless sky. But you went north
because you knew yourself. I tried to imagine
your face, how your singing might sound —
all I could conjure was the night in that damned Camaro,
driving that car like we'd just won it, cruising the peninsula, the neon
     strip
in Niagara Falls, music resonating from the dash.

We waited at a signal, and for some reason,
I looked out the open passenger window
and yelled to a stranger, *"This is not her car!"*
How we laughed,
but still you wouldn't tell me whose car it was.
Now it follows me, a mantra mnemonic of a stupid thing to say.
I can't remember what colour the car was, or even
where we'd been. All our important words

are missing.
I don't know what music was playing — maybe some of that C&W
you'd taught me, strumming your big-body Gibson copy with the sun-
     burst top.
And whose car was it; why was it so funny that you wouldn't say?
We were hysterical over that, that's how our lives were
then.
I remember calling into the faces of strangers.
You were driving.

It was a gorgeous night.
It was not your car.

Shy

Maybe it traces back to that infant moment,
turning blue in the bassinet;
you'd just finished nursing, and something —
    a milky bubble, your first syllable? —
stoppered your throat, you couldn't express, you simply turned blue,
that invisible clot of mother's milk
separating inspiration from expiration until your RN mother noticed
and uncharacteristically panicked, wanted to rush to Emergency

But your father, ever practical, intervened,
asked what she'd do if this happened on the ward,
and so they picked you up by your ankles, held you aloft
upside down and shook you gently through their shaking,
tapped your back with a fleshy palm
    until the viscous bubble split

and half the air of the room,
and all the love they could give
surged to fill you —

flushed with your feeling the first adrenaline rush of the tragic
blooming invisibly inside your body they'd so boldly given life to

Jackknife

Nickel and steel and pearlized blue the colour of lapis:
the jackknife I was allowed to use and pocket
after my father's grave lessons on whittling,
> *Always carve away from your body.*
> *Respect the blade.*
> *Never rest the wood on your knee for leverage.*

How much tender maple or pine did we carve;
patterned nicks, a flat notch for initials, over-exposed
in countless family photos of white sun hats over pixie cuts,
three fair skinned sisters leaning on walking sticks in Canada's
   National Parks,
Fundy, Riding Mountain
                     or Yoho, BC
where another camper asked to try my knife
and after reassuring me in our eight-year-old responsible wisdom
that he knew how to carve,
he sliced the blade expertly down under the bark of a stick
and into the pudgy flesh of his left palm.
                     Dropping the knife,
he took off like a frightened hare.

It took only seconds in slow motion
to retrieve my knife from where it lay glinting, carefully
fold away the blade, then trail the boy screaming toward his campsite
and fetch my mother for moral support. Already his scar
was burning a crimson slash across my hot tears,
gouging deep into my guilty conscience —

His mom had just finished bandaging when my mom
introduced herself to a fellow RN. By now
the boy and I were scared of one another, the wait
grew painful while our mothers talked nursing talk long after our
    apologies.
Back at our campsite, I helped butter bread for noon sandwiches
while the morning scraped over my conscience in faulty repair
and BC mapped on my memory by a red swath through blue sky,
    glimmering —

Flight

I wake up to the sound of a motor
    starting off in the woods outside my tent.
I think *my god she's left me,*
    she's started the Rabbit and she's leaving.
But on my chest, swollen with held breath, I feel her arm
    holding me down against the loose fabric
    and the cold earth.
Last night we broke up, our exasperation
    rising, condensing on the inside of the tent
    trickling down where we stretch the fabric.
It's a grouse, she says, as though she were reading this poem,
    as though she were explaining that the Rabbit would never start,
    that last night we were too tired to fix anything.
The cool morning sun speckles the tent, piling down on our new home.
The motor starts again and I listen
    as she explains the sound,
    her low voice rising through the pillow and into my neck,
Male grouse attract mates by demonstrating
    just how close to flying they can get.

House of Feathers

Winter's cataract
separates like an egg
from the sun's eye.
There's the scent
of singed feathers as I
fall through all my former
houses — dark paradise of
air, trees, earth and water
into the body of something stranger,
more delicate than feathers,
almost human.

I still dream
of bathing by dipping each wing
in water shaking off the drops
like rain when stepping inside
someone else's house.

The Last Words

are for Sava Welsh
who made the best Spanish coffee in the New World,
who gave literally the shirt off his back to a woman
    because she said she liked it,
who worked with me in the bookstore on Robson street
    for most of the thirteen months I've been there,

who worked there for over twenty years,
who used to disappear every Sunday at quarter to five, as he
    said, "like a donkey in the fog",
who would not let his dead mother in once the place
    was locked,

who bought me lunch at Griffins the Friday before he retired
    (we had duck and smoked salmon and desserts that
    would have made a Marxist wince, and Sava ordered
    himself a Spanish coffee, telling the waitress,
    "this could kill me"),
who used to call me "my hero" — I don't know why,
who nursed his lover of over twenty years until he died
    last November, after more than two years of
    sickness,
who thought the card I bought him when Victor died was
    beautiful (thank you, Robert Mapplethorpe)
    and the poem I quoted, too (Langston Hughes),

who retired on a Tuesday in February,
who called me from the back hallway half way through his
    last shift to show the bag full of blood he had
    coughed up,

who smiled when the nurse in the hospital asked me if I was
    his son,
whose liver had been shot for years,
who kept living, I think, for Victor,

who called me from home on a Tuesday evening in March
    to say he was feeling much better and was going
    to fly to Europe in April and would come to see me
    before he went away
who died on the Wednesday of the following week,

who died nearly two months ago now,

who we drank to a month ago in the bar at Griffins, almost
    without mentioning his name, and I went home
    thinking Sava, Sava, Sava,
who disappeared like a donkey in the fog, although I still
    think about him sometimes, Tuesdays, Wednesdays,
    Sundays.

These last words are meant to remember him.
They are not enough.

Who I Was

Driving north in winter twilight,
line of the highway like an open wound
in the snow's chest, the same line
I drove with you
in another, warmer, season.
While you tore over pavement at 160 clicks
we played that game
> *Would you still love me if I had six arms?*
> *If I burned down the library?*
> *If I was an ax murderer?*
pushing the limit of our love
trying to find the place
it would break.

I remember the Rooney Bros. T-shirt
you were wearing, raucous laughter when I asked
If you'd love me if I was a hedgehog,
and I miss you, Matt, that careless confidence,
how recklessly you drove,
sure that we'd never
get caught.

Night settles now, road scabbing over black
like the details of us I can't get at anymore.
Hand on my leg, you were belting out
Elvis Costello,
> *Alison, I know this world is killing you*
> *Alison, my aim is true,*
I remember that, the roar of summer
through the open window
and the promise of an ocean
if only we could drive
fast enough

but I forget who I was
in the passenger seat beside you,
laughing when the cop car finally edged us over,
seat-belt dangling loose at my side.

Up Tunnel Mountain Trail

Laboured, breathless, sweaty. Exposed
roots like ropey veins on the back
of ageing hands. I pause to pant. Up ahead
something small flitters and I see
a chipmunk stand up, strum the Pei Pa. Sun
spangles the drugget of frost on pine needles
scattered like the pick-up-sticks of childhood.
Where do we get the notion that everything
will be all right in the end? Grey flakes of bark
cling to the trunk of the dead, still standing tree
I lean into, feel the brittle, rough rind,
wonder at the will to hold on, how my father
denied anything was wrong, tried to swim
a dozen laps though he'd twice choked
with that dread croaking sound. At the summit
I breathe out into the encircling peaks three huge
OMs echoed by trucks crossing the valley
out of which I've climbed, while in my feet
I feel the start of the slip, the tumble
down the mountain face, hands clutching
at roots, rocks,
straws.

Against the Storm

Low-tide, pretty cobble of entrapment,
a day ends its story with discontent.
Down a mile of shell-shocked beach
oyster farmers push lame shadows
along the watermark, weighted
with buckets, chins to shellfish bed,
crawling the dull edge of the sun.

Muscles in the storm flex and threaten.
Shipwrecked sterling spills and bully-sky
loots every inch of coast around the straight;
pillaged, the horizon weeps,
sundown's flashpoint is swallowed by rain,
twist and grasp from fattening grey.
Oyster-baggers fade in the trouble
of weather, their night bent toward sleep,
tugged anchors, boat-bobbing offshore.

The storm flings the world beyond reach.
Forced from December's black lung
the first breath of winter blasts its victims,
power lines go down in gusts,
explode with rage — the only light
'til match-strike: in isolation,
the islander's plea, waver of candles.

Noon: Cypress Hills

We drive through an oasis in the desert.

A river runs its blue thirst
through sun-torched gorges,

trees named for mourning
crown the sky.

I peel bananas and unwrap
tootsie rolls for lunch,

feed my father as he drives.

My fingers remember his warm mouth,
the countless times
he would carefully bite my hand
and like magic
smile with a sliver between his teeth.

Animals people the landscape,

adolescent mountain goats run up rocks
and cause small avalanches,
cows chew cud like tobacco
in the cheeks of bored baseball players.

My father turns up the music
and Don Williams serenades the bovines.

I look for the bag of intoxicated
green plums that have scented
our van across Saskatchewan.

Every heartache needs to mend
before we love again.

A small calf stares at me
from behind the thin brown
mist in her eyes.

I hold a rancid plum out the window,
an offering that terrifies her
and she backs away shaking

her legs still
fragile as a wishbone.

The Brief Occurrence of Death

I

At the kitchen sink I watch Grandma's fists foam
with the wet silk of Grandpa's hair.

Her breasts brush against his cheek as he traces
a fingernail along the arm of his wheelchair.

A smile begins its long journey across his face
and he breathes in a cocktail of scents:

Coco Chanel on her wrists, lemon floor polish,
summer's last green sigh through the window.

II

Last night as he lay sleeping I watched a halo of pain
open his mouth. There are holes

in his back the size of my palms. Cancer moves through him
deft as a mason. Soon it will leave nothing

but the body's raw-boned trademarks.

III

My mother watches from the table,
suspicious of every passing moment.

For five years she has waited for
the brief occurrence of death to lift Grandpa

out of his wheelchair and walk into the late afternoon light,
draped like an arm across his shoulders.

IV

Outside the wind moves a dry river through the trees.

Grandma tilts his head forward, balancing it
on the stem of his neck. Drops of water rest

on his ears as she talks about planting flowers —
indian paintbrush, tiger lily, snapdragon

the petals, black as burning embers, gently rise
like bulbs in his mind.

And for a moment we lose him
to another season, standing in the garden

a crutch of sunlight to lean on.

Beg and Choose

The burst condom held up
to pale light dripped,
smudged your thighs. I etched
letters into the salt milk,
formed one word.

I prepare for travel,
count backwards
to the last spots of blood.
Am I ovulating now?
— jelly fish sacks open, release
the egg, caught on its path
to the fine velour of the uterus.

I am weighed down
with my backpack, my fear
of carrying a fetus through
foreign countries, the possibility
of misinterpreting morning
sickness for dysentery.

I've already decided; I won't
come home. Will have my belly
blessed by each doubtful
holy man, oiled in jasmine
by long-haired women.
I will birth her without pain,
premature. I will leave her,
slick and brown, in the copper
bowl of a beggar.

Controlled Burn

It was spring and dry, all the snow
retreated to the glaciers and though clouds drifted over
they refused to spill on the backs of the alps.

We hiked in the valley where deer were
tending their fawns and shifting
into parts of the forest that darkened at mid-day;
those overabundant trees seemed to say
no trespassing, this means you
foolish boy. Grow up.

And I was young.

The park rangers lit a fire on the mountain,
a controlled burn to keep the timberland
from torching itself should lightning
or the end of cigarette ignite it.

I explained my naïveté to a woman I'd just met
and said I was so dumb you'd have to
bang me on the head
before I figured out you liked me
you'd have to say something like . . .
"I want to fuck you blind," she said.
Yeah, something like that, I said.

The wind shifted against forecasts
and the fire started leaping back over itself
in the wrong direction. They took to
water-bombing it with helicopters
buzzing the slopes like heavy bees
with their bellies of chemical mist.
All night the mountain glowed,
the end of a mammoth Cuban cigar,
and I leaned out my window
to watch it burn and I smoked a cigarette
the fog lifting from my stunned
pink lungs into the dusk and that
was the beginning of my life.

Lighthouse Route

Easterlies have strewn the open beach
with colander and kelp, but leeward
of the shoals the sands are innocent.
Green crabs venture from the shade
of wrack and rock to promenade
the ripple bottom. Fog slides in,
departs as easily, hiding and exposing
headlands stepping outward to the sea.
White caps wink below the veiled horizon.

We take the cabin for a week away,
with second-hand and hand-me-down,
mismatched sheets and linens,
ancient cookware for an avocado stove;
previous tenants' crafty litter, art
contrived of shells and drift;
for rainy days, old *Maclean's*
and *Chatelaines*, two decks of cards,
one missing both red queens,
a hi-fi with a broken changer,
tube-type tuner whistling
over static and short wave.

On the tide-line trash, a seagull
caters to a fat, brown chick
that cringes, whinges, *"Me! Me!"*
She cries to the sky, *"Why? Why?"*
"'Cause, 'cause," the lofty crows reply.
On a rocky lip a scoter drake
oversees his flightless flock,
and cormorants hang out to dry.

A beer can hisses, snaps and punctuates
the slow sweep of the low swell. Men
in muscle shirt and ripe round belly,
toughened by a mean sea
and reluctant land, cut mackerel.
(A dozen gulls glean after them.)
Women here grow hard as well,
against the burden of the men.

Grasshoppers clatter by, superb in gilt
and sable, keepers of the summer day.
Between the sea fog and the thunderheads,
our highway in the sunshine overlies
primaeval paving stones, worn smooth
and closely fitted, like old love.

Green Bay, Nova Scotia,
September 1999

Back on the Road to Bakersfield

In our little kitchen, my mother
sang. The radio played, potatoes boiled, bread
rose, the tea pot stayed on and the laundry
was ironed — load after load after . . . It is 1960
something, Buck Owens is singing,
     They're gonna put me in the movies
     They're gonna make a big star outta me . . .
Mother is tapping her foot, the steam is
rising. And we became every chorus, every
note, every heartache and when Billy Joe McAllister
jumped off the Tallahatchie Bridge the sorrow
was sweet. It was Don Messer and Ed
Sullivan. It was Dean Martin and Johnny
Cash and I learned to dance. Round and

round the little kitchen until somewhere
between Buck Owens and Loretta Lynn, Chuck
Berry taught us to twist,
     Let's twist again like we did . . .
In the little kitchen that shone even at
midnight, music ministered. But with Dylan we
parted company, my mother and I, *"My word,"*
she'd say, *"you can't keep time to that."* And
I would shrug, LSD and Dylan were not about
"keeping time." I laughed at The Buckaroos, at the
corny, unsophisticated lyrics, at the cowboys in
sequins, never letting on that The Tennessee
Waltz could still make me cry until
her eyes clouded and her body failed and I
returned. I would go see her, the little
kitchen long gone, to sit with her, "keep
time" and drink tea and every Saturday evening

she would have the operator dial my
number, every Saturday 7:00 p.m., to say, *"The
After Supper Breakdown's on, dear heart,"* and every
Saturday at 7:00 p.m., I would say, *"Thanks, Mum, I'll
turn it on right away,"* and never did. Now time
had moved us further into last chances and ruined
remains and we do not "keep time" anymore. There
are no songs. A dark impregnable abyss covers
her mind. The last bastion has crumbled — a steel
guitar and a rising fiddle are now only awful
agonies. But when I come home to my
rose coloured parlour, I play Dwight, see a woman
and a little girl orbit a yellow light and when
my children complain, cry, *"Aw Mum, Dwight Yoakam?
even Tom Waits is better that this."* How can I tell
them about this small salvation, how can I explain that
"keeping time" for both of us, is the only way
I have left to hold on.

The Writing Room

The caretaker shows me a room
I can rent by the hour.
He smells of gin, doesn't know I have two kids
waiting in the car, so he makes his moves.

Mother says what goes around comes around.
She tells me *never ever shave your legs.*
Why live with regret? Buys me a box of clay,
says God made the world, see what you can do.

I can afford a room badly lit,
a tiny bed, suffering.
Artists never make good prisoners.
They know what to do with their hands.

I tie my children to the fire hydrant.
Tell them they must be patient with Mommy.
She will be back. They must imagine her coming back.

Moortown Errata*

In line 10 of "Night arrival of Sea-trout",
    for "rape", read "nape" —
as though you might believe it possible
    to plunge yourself
    into a trout
and have her turn away from love
    forever. The men
of Moortown have never read
    a poem, but know
love, her body and shine slashing
    through the almost frozen
Moortown river. Each morning they
    abandon wife
and lover to wait in a silence that wraps
    their bones as tin
foil wraps a baked potato. They know
    she will arrive,
the woman they cannot enter, breaking
    the river's smoking surface,
    too hungry for words.

---

* The first two lines of this poem owe themselves to an appended list of errata
found in Ted Hughes' collection of poems titled *Moortown*.

Karaoke

A man is singing karaoke
in the seabus terminal.
His voice is a loud ghost's
and the gaping in the air
as the ghost moves out
among the commuters
waiting for the next sailing
which will take them home
across the deep waters
steely in the late fall light.
An odd voice, and artless,
but smooth, rich beneath
the hoarse, breaking surface
(the mouth it comes out of
palsied and awry, forming
all its words at an angle,
the face distorted, always
turned up off to the side),
it sings of love and love lost,
some sugary sad pop song,
yet really sings it.
One of his arms, ruined,
with a kind of flipper hand,
jerks across his chicken chest,
and every few bars
he snaps down and lays
his torso on his stick thighs,
still singing and smiling
while his head is hanging down
at his wheelchair footrests.
He accepts a ten dollar bill
from a woman, shifting
his mouth away from the mike

and talking, asking her
to take change from the case
lying open in front of him.
The song's tinny backbeat
and muzak melody continue on
without him, pouring out
of his portable p.a. system,
and out of the wheelchair
and the deformed body,
the ingenious half-machine
invention of himself.
Now I turn to him
as I put a pay phone down.
The seabus is rumbling
into its berth to a buzzer sound,
and a couple of people
are throwing a last few coins
into the money case.
The sun rays in through glass
and makes the souls of everyone
in the terminal visible
for an instant, and the souls
truly hear the wailing voice.
Listen to the reed, it cries,
and the pain in the tale it tells
of being cut from the reed bed,
how it sings of separation
from its home in any gathering.

Vancouver

Your Keys

for my grandfather

In the last year or two of your life,
you were always asking for your keys.
Every few minutes, it seemed: *"Where are my keys?"*
Bewildered-looking, and not remembering
you'd asked the same thing dozens of times that day,
frightened-looking, a child's desperation
shooting across your child's wide eyes.
"You don't need them," we'd tell you.
But we were wrong; you needed them all right.
You wanted your life back,
and were holding on with whatever delicate
and near-miraculous, harried energy you still had
to the days of house and apartment doors,
and were imagining locking and unlocking
every minute left to you now
while you paced and circled in the always-unlocked
last room you'd live in, waiting to be taken out
for hallway walks or downstairs meals,
then impatient to come back again, and be there again
alone with her, in the minutes you still knew
you'd forget almost as soon as they passed.
And so when you were cremated, we had an old set
put in your coffin with you in your shirt pocket.
I remembered you years before —
before strokes and memory loss and dementia:
you and my grandmother
in the Sears cafeteria in the mall
having dishwater coffee and worse soup together.
She'd gone to get serviettes,
and you turned to me and said,
"You know, this is all I want. It's funny."

I thought not much about it then.
I was twenty, maybe. But now, fifteen years or so later,
I think that in your way you were handing me a key.
And now I wish you your ring of keys back in your hand
and all your memory safe, intact and shining,
and more if there is anything more.

Helen's Room

This probably isn't what Virginia meant
by a room of one's own, furnace at my back
and a poster (*The Lady's Not for Burning*),
grey walls hardly visible
behind the books and filing cabinets,
my sewing desk, the washing machine,
bulletin boards layered with must-do lists
grown musty

(All that's missing is the mildew,
but a girl can't have everything!)

A room in the underworld
isn't quite what I intended either,
but here I am, encrypted
with the mealy bugs and spiders,
closed in with my heart's stationary wanderings

Reminds me of a mausoleum, this place,
certainly a tomb of one type or another;
which means there are treasures too,
necessities for the during-life

What I cherish most: the gifts from my children,
rocks, driftwood, imprints of their childhood
like the hand my youngest gave me,
green fingers, red palm
pressed into white plaster

I survey the clutter:
open texts, papers at my feet,
notes scattered like landmines,
one small window only, sealed

I wish often for light,
possibly an explosion;
anything to help me breathe

But there are compensations:
frogs' bellies pressed against the glass,
field mice scurrying to their destinies,
thoughts about sky

The Bath

for my brother, an alcoholic, who at
the age of twenty-seven, drowned in a pool

The girl watches her mother
set out the basin,
dip her elbow, testing the water
for the new baby's bath.

Mother, I had a strange dream.
I saw white hands floating like soap.

Wind rattles the windows
but the kitchen is warm;
the wood stove has a stomachful
of crackling pine; on the oven door
the mother heats a clean towel.
Something to wrap him in.

All that night, he lay alone on the bottom.

The baby sprawls on his mother's lap
displaying his watered-silk skin
and, below the pot belly,
          his bud like a rose.

Mother, I saw white hands
          floating like lilies.

The mother murmurs.
The little girl hovers; she can't stop
beaming, she's in love. She laughs
at the funny bent legs drawn up
like a Sunday roast chicken's,
tries to capture the fluttering feet.
Hold them: two soft velvet mice.

Nocturne

Usually,
at this time of day,
I move from room to room
pulling blinds, switching on lamps.

It is not the dark,
but the slow drain of light
that I can't bear, the way
things must become half-seen
before they disappear.

Tonight,
some invisible hand holds me
in place, fastens
the soft gathers of night
around me. I see

the dinner dishes
on the kitchen counter, littered
with bones and rinds,
the muddy running shoes
with ragged tongues, discarded
at the door, begin to lose their edges.

Tonight,
shadow forgives everything —
as fond of the careless leavings of our day,
as of the white throats of lilies.

This August evening, I almost believe
that dusk is the only merciful delivery
into night.

The Shock

When my grandmother was six months pregnant
with her first child
her husband was lost at sea.

According to my aunts
she stepped onto the trolley car
one fall afternoon, oblivious,
read the headline
over the shoulder of the man in front of her:
"Canadian Exporter Disappeared."

The ship was bound for Australia from Vancouver
with a bellyful of Doug fir.
Three weeks out, the cargo shifted
and the engine room flooded.

I don't know whether she cried
right there on the trolley,
whether she turned pale and got off at the next stop,
stood there looking out to sea,
not noticing the child turning.

If she were alive now
I would ask her how she felt
when her husband was rescued
from a lifeboat, fifteen days later
off the coast of California.

I would ask her about the baby,
whether it was the shock
that left the subtle scars
my father bore as man —
that made him disappear over and over
and always drift back.

My Neighbour's Work

Minutes before
the thunderstorm,
my neighbour goes into her garden
to rescue the peonies.

Their pink and white
billowy heads are weighted
with the worries of saints.
Tremulous visions
of wind and destruction.

Soon, she will leave
for her job at the library.
Gather books to take
to the prison.

As the late afternoon light
is turning front lawns
into gilded pages,

my neighbour will walk
down prosaic halls
where even the shadows
are preordained, and fall
warily through the metal slats
of blinds and bars,

her freckled arms
ladened with books.
Words burning
to be released.

For three hours
every week, she will study
the cryptic narration of lines
scrawled at the corners
of lips and eyes,
try to decipher
what is to be read there.

At suppertime, she will return
to the quiet house
of her husband's gaze,
place wine and bread
on her wooden table

and watch
the sun through
the kitchen window,
bowing its bloody head
into the ground.

The storm
a faintly-heard conversation:
music from another room.

Trying, still,
to take her attention
from all that ties her
to this world,

from the light
that will not
leave her hands.

Cotton

The summer we were Tom and Huck
out father bought a packet of seeds.
He wanted us to understand
the South: what cotton did to the land
and the people on it. *Takes rivers*
he said as he turned on the hose. *Wears out the soil*
as he sprinkled Vigoro from a bag.

Did he show us where to plant, and how
deep? We were dreaming up a river
for our raft. Who hoed and weeded,
between his Sweetheart roses? We tightroped
the white board fence, one foot, one foot,
above his history lesson.

I do remember the pale saucer flowers,
the powderpuffs we twisted
from the knife-
edged sepals. *Slavery* he said. *Stoop labour.*
No way could two children's fingers
ever pick that jagged seed clean.

            *   *   *

I have been to southeastern India, seen
the flat fields, the dugouts for water,
haze in the middle distance pooling
at the hems of bright saris. But

this is not a travel poster.

Andhra Pradesh looks like cotton country.
Here is the salesman, his car
tanked on promises. Here are the farmers
who could do with a little cash.
Whole villages go for it, and why
not? A cottonfield in bloom is a beautiful sight (pale
saucer flowers). Bugs beyond counting agree.

Bottles with skull and crossbones
arrive with the shipment of seed.
The farmers upend the bottles onto the grub
that tunnels the cotton's sweet heart,
that pays no mind to crossbones and moves on

to carrots and beans.
Now what to do?
One by one, in one small district, up
to their necks in debt, fifty-three farmers down
the poison themsélves.
Dust blows over the dry
stalks, whispering *history, history.*

To the Father at the Beach

You're scaring me. You're scaring
my granddaughter, not to mention
the shorebirds and this boy
who won't wear shoes — your arc of terror,
your *why do you always?*

See how small he is. Think
how small he'll look when he leaves,
the way my son left, lifting
a pack onto his hollow bones, and I didn't
run after him, didn't notice
the sharp-eyed streets or the shadows
going *Psst. Over here.*

Maybe your son will forgive.
Mine says he does, or rather
that forgiveness isn't called for, but
this is not about guilt, it's to do with attention.

Haven't you heard the bear and cougar stories
they're swapping back in the village?
Let's keep ourselves on the upland side
of these children. Whatever lurks in the forest
will have to deal with us first.

Drunk

I knew what I had to do when I saw him
lurching toward me across the front lawn.
Mend the hole in my heart, he might have sung
to the wild geese flying over our heads.
I felt for his keys in my back pocket.
His wife, that lovely Scottish girl,
stood in front of the Valiant,
arms crossed like a prison guard's.
And when he tripped over his feet,
the stiff fingers of the wind
caught him before he fell. It was late
and the children peered out the rear window.
I could see it in his eyes: nothing would stop him.
He *would* drive that car down the starlit
highway, he loved those kids so much
he *would* stumble deeper
and deeper into the broken world.
Dae it, dae it, the woman shouted at me,
her dress stained with blueberries,
the hopeless future careening toward her.
Was it good advice? I don't know
but a fist swam out of my sleeve and he fell to the ground.
I might have said, *brother, let's sit on the grass
and talk of those long afternoons
we cast our lines into the river.* I might have
kissed his forehead before knocking him
out cold, I might have turned
to the children
who for years afterwards
would roll their eyes, the whites
whiter than the white of a hooked fish belly.

Spotter

Above your head
a boy straddles the high bar.
He is talking himself into something,
his latest trick, a name like a drink:
rigor mortis,
double with a twist.

You plant your feet, extend your arms,
anticipate distance, weight.
The instructor says you are here
to absorb impact, to crumple if necessary
like the fender of a car.
You think of your neighbour in his new
Fairlane, the acres of chrome
and the green wings that carry him
to work.
You think of the friends who stood by and
watched you trade twenty dollars
for five hits of window pane,
how they cheered when you swallowed three at once,
talking you through
the long night and day that followed.

There is no end to all this sacrifice,
to the things we place between ourselves
and disaster.
The seat belts, the life jackets, the steel
guard that directs the carving knife away
from your father's wrist.
It occurs to you that every moment you are alive
is an exercise in trust.

And when the boy's hands finally fail,
his body spinning toward you like a pilot
shot out of his doomed plane,
you lower him carefully onto the sea of blue
tumbling mats,
words already forming on your lips,
consolation, a tip on technique,
whatever it takes to get him up,
try again.

The Canadian Youth Competition

SENIOR DIVISION

Introduction to the Senior Division

Judges: Jannie Edwards, Christopher Wiseman

When it comes to choosing the actual winners and putting poems from a 20-odd poem short list in rank order, a certain arbitrariness is inevitable. We both had our choices for these positions, and, in the end, it became reasonably easy to come up with a list, though it meant omitting poems we both liked and comparing chalk with cheese. A few things we can say about the six poems chosen are that, in general, they are more completed, more unusual, more vital than the vast majority of the 1,500 poems we read.

Sharon Page's "Water Buffalo + Emily = Love" is a good example of the fresh and unusual. We had never seen a poem quite like it in its mixing of wonderfully bizarre images which both surprise and delight and demonstrate a rich imagination, a child-like vision, a great sense of humour, a sophisticated use of language and a fine economy. The first line "Emily Fraser loves water buffalo" is a classic; when it leads to "because they don't use toilet paper", it becomes sublimely, ridiculously pleasing. And the pace doesn't flag, leading, as it does, to the cryptic, perfect ending, where Mrs. Steida can only suggest therapy because she can't understand the world of Emily's creative imagination.

"The Deluge" by Mike Mulley works well because of its understated depiction of the mother with her "swollen arm" who counterpoints brilliantly the father and child who throw the skipping rocks so freely. All she can wait for is the deluge, the threat, the thing she's dreaded all her life. This is a wonderful example of saying a great deal without spelling it out. The very air around the stricken mother is "bitter" and the time is "too late." Cleanly and confidently written, this poem is moving and powerful.

Robin Daniels' "Tea at High Acre, When I Was a Boy" takes us comprehensively and delightfully into another world of both place and time. Rarely do you see a poem dealing with memory from a young person which convinces this way. The poem teems with concrete details of landscape, people, activities, animals, food, nature, but it's the human observer who must bring all these together, and that's done here by the superb final image of the tea leaves "preserved in cold / sweet honey / like these memories." We both thought this poem was stunning in its detail and yet it never goes too far into travelogue before it's pulled back to the human.

Emily Rosser's "someone breathing evenly" is a poem of great skill and even more promise. We found the first paragraph a little easy, a bit more clichéd than the rest; otherwise this could have been even higher placed. (In fact, the poem might well begin with the second paragraph.) A meditation on intense isolation and feelings of disconnection, the poem moves actively around and enhances the subject. And for someone this young to be writing lines like "But I like it there, the backward slide and the / perfect escape into / chilled   thin   air" or "everything is the right size, / the right distance from happening" struck us as remarkable, and the final lines are simply excellent.

Leah Todd's "The First Time" pleases us because of its avoidance of the obvious in this far from original subject. The use of the Halloween story — the girl feeling too old, smoking a cigarette, being rejected as too old, yet still going around doing children's things — moves smoothly into the sudden onset of womanhood. And the use of the mother, beautifully portrayed at the start and end of the poem, gives the experience a moving architecture. It would have been easy to write "took my fingers / and kissed them" at the end. Ninety-nine out of one hundred poets at this level would have. This very talented and promising poet writes "took the bones of my fingers / and kissed them." All the difference in the world. As with the reference to David Lanz — such lovely particularity.

Sascha Braunig's "Family Reunion" doesn't hold back, and we loved its rich humanity. The aunts seem subordinate, somehow, in terms of excitement (the cousins smoking pot; the uncles talking hockey) but it's deceptive. The aunts are the ones who've lived, even though they sit and drink and talk: "four birds with smoky halos." They are the ones who've had bad marriages and bad kids. And, finally, at the end of this finely turned and economical poem, they are seen for the great characters they are. Unlike the hockey jocks, they are the ones who "know the score." And the poet impressed us with her ability to show that so clearly and well.

These six, then, are the ones we chose to fill the winning places, but we want to insist on mentioning some other poems, if only to tell the authors that they were all, from time to time, in our deliberations, considered for the top spots, and that we think they are winners, too, in their own ways. Perhaps it was just a weakness in a line or two, or a mixup in a point of view, or a sentimental image, or a weak ending that bothered us, but the following poems impressed us greatly and were really part of the winning six: "Baby Autumn", "the writer", "Nicknames That Make Sailors Blush", "A Lazy Bee Poem For Martin", "Sean", "Bus Tickets for Vince", "The Black Miniskirts", "The Clowns", "Just Ask Me", "Legacy" and others it would take too long to mention. You are all winners in our eyes, and your poems are not "worse" than the six we called winners. Just perhaps a little less far along, or with some small problem. That's 16 poems out of approximately 1,500. You should all be very proud, and we would both urge you to keep trying, keep writing poems, keep reading poems (at least 20 for every one you write), keep working to get your imaginative visions down on paper the best you can. There is so much promise in your work, and so much life and buoyancy and vitality.

— Jannie Edwards and
Christopher Wiseman

The Canadian Youth Competition
Senior Division Prize Winners

FIRST PRIZE
Sharon Page
"Water Buffalo + Emily = Love"

SECOND PRIZE
Mike Mulley
"The Deluge"

THIRD PRIZE
Robin Daniels
"Tea at High Acre, When I Was a Boy"

HONOURABLE MENTIONS
Leah Todd, Victoria, BC, "The First Time"
Sascha Braunig, Victoria, BC, "Family Reunion"
Emily Rosser, Georgetown, Ontario, "someone breathing evenly"

Water Buffalo + Emily = Love

Emily Fraser loves water buffalo
because they don't use toilet paper
or shampoo or put violets
in film canisters
like she does for Mother's Day.

In kindergarten the fort I made with her
was in the blackberry bushes
(water buffalo stake out their territory)
fascinating tunnels along the neighbour's fence
where we hid
a collection of dolls' shoes
and bottle caps.

At the end of recess
we got bloody fingers on prickles
(water buffalo don't use bandaids).
(They don't like mustard or
Barbie backpacks.)

Emily draws pictures of them
in her journal
blobs of brown crayon
against deserted hills and zebra grass.
Beat up a kid once
for the blue felt
(water buffalo lock horns over hollows of muck).

At parent-teacher interviews
Mrs. Steida suggests therapy.

The Deluge

By the ocean
we skip rocks,
my father's wrist
flicking like a trigger,
shooting the smooth, flat bullet
into the water. He calls out
the number of each hop,
until the water's skin is pierced
at seven.

My mother is next,
her swollen arm
swinging uselessly
against the bitter air
so that when the rock hits,
it sinks, a splash,
a sudden wave.
She jumps back
to avoid the spray,
but is too late

and starts to accuse
us, the water,
the cold, salty drops
burning her skin,
doesn't see the
small ripples,
only the big wave coming,
sweeping over the shore,
just as she has imagined it
since the day she was born.

Tea at High Acre, When I Was a Boy

Dust hangs heavy in the air from the
gravel driveway.
Mrs. Wilson's three dogs yap at passers,
guarding the bushveld
of her garden.

We sit, cool, under the shady boughs of the old
jacaranda. Gnarled limbs reach up,
twisted, to grapple at the blood
and ruby-breasted
"piet-my-vrou" tinkering and
piping overhead.
Grandpa Geoff planted the jacaranda
forty years ago.

A hug from Granny Aimee,
warm, a soft, scented coat
of brown sugar and rosemary
crisp toast and apple honey
blanket my tongue.

Talk of rhododendrons and azaleas
waft over my head.
I don't listen because the garlic crusher
and I are digging,
for diamonds, in the butter's
misty depths. Just like Grandpa Errol
in his mine. A shaky hand,
laced with purple faults summons me
to my muesli,
sour yoghurt on the summit
halting the excavation.

The jacaranda droops in the
midday heat.
Leaves choking with
dust.
Tea leaves settled
at the bottom of our empty teacups
preserved in cold
sweet honey
like these memories.

The First Time

My mother always told me
when it happened we would
have dinner on Broadway
or go shopping and pick something out
in the women's section.
Halloween, 1994:
twelve years old, two long braids
clear skin, bony as hell
frigid air and firecrackers
the smell of burning leaves.
I was kicking chestnuts,
cigarette glowing
a weighty bag of candy
rejected from doorsteps because I looked too old
in the eyes of disapproving baby boomers.
Home again, I pulled down my underwear
incredulous before the sudden, intense red
upon clean cotton.
My mother was playing David Lanz on her piano,
a sad piece.
I dangled my underwear for her to see.
She released the keys
went quiet,
took the bones of my fingers
and kissed them.

Family Reunion

My aunts
Wizened booze-hounds
Drain their glasses
And sing drily,
Cracked, black-haired and garish.
They are four birds with smoky halos.
Their failed marriages and delinquent children
Trail behind them like mascara.
I sit amazed at their wrinkled
Drunken glory.
My cousins smoke pot
Ask me, *"How was your trip?"*
My uncles
Discuss hockey,
Rub nicotined hands.
They can only shift their sad sacks of flesh around
While my aunts croon
Cackle and wheeze
They know the score.

someone breathing evenly

The air grows cold and it spits rain while the sun is out,
and things fall slowly into place without
my noticing.
I slept forever today
rolled over and shrank away from daylight sharpness
back into a
soft cocoon,
sifting through dreams where I am old or
flying,
where I am always in control.

Cold but true
I crept up, made coffee at two
and drank it thinking of what I would
otherwise be doing
and as I sat,
   I was real, and things were going right.

I smell the fires,
I know winter is coming,
   and maybe I'm introverting
   but I like it there, the backward slide and the
perfect escape into
chilled   thin   air

I am regaining sight
in the violent colours of dying leaves
outside, where the world is becoming breathable again
and everything is the right size,
the right distance from happening

in the hissing of ice crystals forming on puddles
I hear the absence of voices

and the almost silent but unmistakeable
   brakes of time
    slowing to my pace.

The Canadian
Youth Competition

JUNIOR DIVISION

Introduction to the Junior Division

Judges: Richard Harrison, Gwen Molnar

It is our great pleasure to present the following ten winners and honourable mentions in the junior category. These are not "youth poems"; these are poems of the young. They don't try to be other than the words of our children using the language they know in the best way they can. Paradoxically, perhaps, it's their very youth-fullness, that lets them step beyond their years and be set beside other works as "poems" alone. They offer us reflections on life and death, the meaning of self, the love of unloved things, the power of nature and the consequences of social inequity.

These new and forming voices speak joyfully, or in pain; in fear or in wonder; they tell us their story slant, or direct themselves to our ears with the tone of the plain-spoken truth. We are happy to recommend them to you.

The winning poems will speak for themselves, but we also want to let you know what we found in the entries as a whole. Much of the writing, as you'd imagine, is filled with what those who are happy to have finished with them call "growing pains", both in terms of what they are saying and how they are saying it.

Being a child is no less easy or free of anguish today than it was 10 or 20 or 30 years ago. It is still a time of loneliness and longing for the love of family and peers, of questioning what makes friendship, and of learning that even the most intensely desired relationships and ideas don't last the forever they're supposed to. It is still a time of searching for expression.

But what opened our eyes as well as touched our hearts was how much of the adult world our children see and react to. If the thousand poems we read say anything to us as adults, it's this: you're not getting away with anything. More than you might think, we feel the deaths of the victims of war even though most of us have never known them ourselves. We are burdened already with the responsibility to do better. We are touched by death and we have lost friends, too. We worry about the violence that clouds our school lives. And speaking of that, we know the difference between being schooled and being taught. We know when you cheat on each other. We want to be accepted. What makes us happy can be just as profound as what brings you joy. When you reject us, we feel it more than we let show.

Like all poets, our children are keenly aware of the power of language, and they are measuring us, too, against our words even as we are reading theirs.

— Richard Harrison
and Gwen Molnar

The Canadian Youth Competition
Junior Division Prize Winners

FIRST PRIZE
Michael Coren
"The Graveyard"

SECOND PRIZE
Katie Dawn English
"There Upon a Lumpy Rock"

THIRD PRIZE
Jennifer Patterson
"Troubled Boys"

HONOURABLE MENTIONS
Claire Haddock, Port Moody, BC,
"Cleaning My Rat's Cage", "Old Growth", "Wind"
Jessica Brohart, Renfrew, Ontario, "Inside Out"
Shannon Downs, Passekeag, New Brunswick, "Youth"
Helen Beynon, Burnaby, BC, "Shoe Store"
Allanda Jean Carter, Qualicum Beach, BC, "To a Daughter"

The Graveyard

I sit among graves
All filled by war and conflict
What can one boy do?

There Upon a Lumpy Rock

There upon a lumpy rock
Sits a lady, crippled in fright.
I hear her soft cries for money.
I hand her a few coins and tell her,
"It won't buy you happiness."

Troubled Boys

They were like tornadoes;
Unpredictable,
Disastrous.

They were like the dark;
Sad,
Depressed,
Secretive.

They were troubled boys
Who could have looked
Into the future and seen
Everything would be all right.

They didn't.
They couldn't.

Bottled up emotions and
Problems
Released in many bangs.

The other children
Never knew
How their taunts and teases
Troubled the boys.

They finally knew
After the tornado had stopped whirling
They finally knew
After the dark skies
Had delivered their storms.

Cleaning My Rat's Cage

I snap off the hinges
and open the lid
lifting the metal bars
to watch a pink nose
emerge from its box.

A sour smell radiates
from old sawdust.
A plump body wiggles out
and a tail that none likes
but me, dragging behind.

I lift the cage to the sink
and dump the dirty bits
into the garbage,
open the new bag of pinechips.
The cage towers over her
like a building.

Bubbles form
as I pour stale water
from her container
and fill it with new.

The cheese house
has to be rearranged
for her majesty
who demands for a snack
tiny rodent chocolates
in a small white dish.

This is her home,
the safe place
she always has to return to.

Old Growth

Mossy clumps of ferns
fill the air.
Old and wise trees
stand up tall
looking down at us.

As we die
old growth is still growing,
growing, for another
thousand years.

Wind

Fierce as a mad bear,
the wind tears rose's petals,
flinging them on rocks.

Inside Out

listening, I was listening to a cold wind,
a harsh tone
then, a voice
try to change, it says, you only have two choices
the voice was familiar, I had heard it before.
when I asked who it was, the voice replied sadly
"I am experience"
I've done what you're doing. I've seen what it does
I'm telling you what happens, what it will do
it won't happen to me
a bad attitude
the voice was gone
when I looked up, there stood a girl just like a picture
outlined by a wooden frame.
identical to me, only backwards
she didn't speak
I looked away, preparing to turn myself inside out
and then I was fine

Youth

Young children are called youth.
They like flowers because flowers are colourful.
They come in all shapes and sizes,
Just like children do.
When children are outside and playing,
They see flowers all around them.
And some children go and pick them.
But it's too late.
The school bell has rung time to go and learn.

Shoe Store

Rows of sandals line
the wall.
Flats, Flip Flops, Strappy platforms.
I reach for the sequined stilettos,
and pull them close to my face.
Her arm encircles my hunched shoulders.
She murmurs in my ear,
and I pull away
"You're too good for those,"
she says.
"We can afford much better.
Why settle for those?
They don't suit you."
I shake my head, asking for
size 10.
The salesman sighs.
They only have size 9.
I cram my foot into the
glittering shoe.
It seems to snicker at me.
"You'll never get that giant into me,"
it says.
She stands in front of me,
tapping her foot in exasperation.
"Let's go. We can find something much nicer in
the shoe store next door."
I hold back the tears,
and drop the shoes back into their
tattered cardboard box.
I feel my finely manicured nails
digging painfully into the palm of my hand,
as she struts out the entrance,
her air of sophistication polluting

the atmosphere around her.
The cashier murmurs to her friend,
as I follow the queenly woman out the door,
"Rich snobs."
I wince.
The woman grabs my hand and pulls me along
the crowded corridor.
"You have to learn to accept your money, darling.
When are you ever going to
change?"

To a Daughter

Do you know you're beautiful

I don't mean that as a cheap one-liner
Or as a romantic compliment
I mean it as an honest question
I'm curious
Do you know you're beautiful?

I only ask because
You're beautiful enough to know it
And be proud of it
And use it
Beautiful enough to put yourself on a pedestal
To walk with your chin held high
And your head in the sky
To pass by the ugly people
Without so much as a word
Or a glance.

But you don't
And I love you for it.

I love the way you walk
With your head cast down
Or bent to one side
Unjudging
High shoulders slightly slumped
Deep eyes with nothing to hide
Unpresuming.

I love the way you walk without a pedestal
Among the ugly people
Right at home
As if you don't know that you stand out
Like the first bright star on the black sea
Or a light-house beacon high in the night sky

Do you know you're beautiful?

It's funny, though
Ironic
That in not putting yourself on that pedestal
I have put you on one of my own
A higher one
For being so gracious
So real
So beautiful

Do you know you're beautiful

You really don't do you

Beautiful

TAMMY ARMSTRONG's poetry has been published or accepted for publication in *Room of One's Own, The Fiddlehead, Event, TickleAce, The Antigonish Review, Sub-Terrain,* and *Pottersfield Portfolio.* Currently she is finishing a poetry manuscript entitled "A Proper Burial for Songbirds."

HELEN BEYNON enjoys the arts. Her favourite things to do are drawing, painting and writing. She has written many short stories and poems for school competitions and just for fun. She also enjoys rugby and figure skating.

SASCHA BRAUNIG is sixteen years old. She plans to pursue a career combining visual arts and writing. Please hire her.

STEPHEN BROCKWELL published *The Wire in Fences* in 1988. A new collection, *The Cometology,* will appear in 2000 from ECW Press. His work has appeared in numerous anthologies and journals, such as *Descant, Canadian Literature, Prism international* and *The Fiddlehead.*

JESSICA BROHART is a grade nine student at R.C.I. Her work has been published once before. She enjoys poetry and writing in her spare time.

ALLANDA JEAN CARTER is a thirteen-year-old girl who's into art, Japanese anime, drawing, hanging out with her friends and writing. She loves nature and what goes with it. She likes to express herself through art and writing.

MICHAEL COREN lives in Langley, B.C. He is twelve years old and attends the Southridge school in Surrey, B.C.

LAURA CUDWORTH is a graduate of the creative writing programme at York University. She was raised by her grandparents in Weston, Ontario, and now resides in Guelph.

ROBIN DANIELS, a Claremont Secondary school student in Victoria, B.C., recently moved from South Africa. His interests are mountain biking, wind surfing and hiking. He has won several awards: English (Platinum), Math (Gold), National Olympiad Science Fair (Silver).

SHANNON DOWNS lives in Passekeag, New Brunswick. She was born in Saint John and has grown up mostly in Hampton. She is twelve years old, likes to learn about history, and to babysit.

KATIE DAWN ENGLISH is involved in two different sports, in which she has won many awards, including the grade sixers' community involvement award. This is the first poem she has entered in the contest.

DAVID FREEMAN recently won second prize and $500 at the Festival of Words in Moose Jaw, Saskatchewan, for a poem entitled "The Hunt." Currently he is looking for a poetry publisher for a manuscript entitled "A Collection of Stones."

CLAIRE HADDOCK is in grade seven of the Fraser Valley Distance Education programme. She lives in Port Moody, B.C. and is interested in drumming, music and animal rights. She was awarded the second prize in the Remembrance Day Literary Contest at Parkland Elementary School in grade six.

JENNICA HARPER is a poet and a screenwriter whose work has appeared, or is forthcoming, in *Geist, Descant, The Antigonish Review, The Seattle Review* and *Room of One's Own*. In 1997, she won the E.J. Pratt Prize for poetry. Jennica has an MFA in Creative Writing from the University of British Columbia.

GARY HYLAND heads ArtSchool Saskatchewan, the Festival of Words and Moose Jaw Arts in Motion. He has two books of poetry in print: *After Atlantis* (Thistledown), and *White Crane Spreads Wings* (Coteau Books). His poems have appeared in many journals and three previous editions of *Vintage*. He lives in Moose Jaw.

JOCKO is the author of one collection of poetry, *An Anarchist Dream*. His poems have appeared in magazines in Canada, the U.S. and Australia. He does not own any plants — even the ones that appear in his poems die on him.

EVE JOSEPH was born in North Vancouver, and currently lives in Brentwood Bay with her children. She is a counselling psychologist and works at the Victoria Hospice.

FIONA TINWEI LAM is a Scottish born, Vancouver-based writer of poetry and fiction. Her poems have been published in *Contemporary Verse II, The Antigonish Review, Whetstone, Canadian Literature, The Literary Review of Canada, White Wall Review, The New Quarterly, Bite,* and the anthology *A Room at the Heart of Things* (Véhicule Press) with two more forthcoming in *Descant.* Ten poems are included in *Swallowing Clouds,* an anthology of Chinese Canadian poetry (Arsenal Pulp Press, 1999).

NANCY LEE is an award-winning fiction writer and poet. Her work has appeared in literary journals across Canada. She recently completed her MFA in Creative Writing at the University of British Columbia.

Saskatoon writer SHELLEY A. LEEDAHL enjoys the challenge of writing in various genres. Her books include *The Bone Talker* (children's picture book, Red Deer press, 1999); *Riding Planet Earth* (juvenile novel, Roussan Publishers, 1997); *Sky Kickers* (adult short stories, Thistledown Press, 1994); and *A Few Words for January* (poetry, Thistledown Press, 1990). A novel is forthcoming (fall 2000), and a second book of poetry will be published in 2001.

SUE MACLEOD lives in Halifax, where she works part time in a public library. Some of her recent poems have appeared in *The Fiddlehead, Grain* and *The Malahat Review.*

KAREN MASSEY's poetry has appeared in various Canadian literary publications and anthologies including *Written in the Skin* (Insomniac Press), *Vintage 97/98* (Quarry Press), and *Shadowy Technicians: New Ottawa Poets* (Broken Jaw Press). Her chapbook *Bullet* is from above/ground press. She received an MA in English literature from Concordia University, and now lives in Ottawa working as an artisan.

SPENCER MAYBEE was born in Toronto, reborn in Victoria and reborn again in the Alberta foothills west of Edmonton. He writes poetry, fiction, screen drama and nonfiction. He won the Milen Scholarship for writing in 1998 and the 1996 Toronto Council of Teachers of English Short Story Award. He was guest publisher for *Inner Harbour Review* 1997–1999 and has been published in the *Inner Harbour Review* and *Leaving Juvenilia,* a chapbook of University of Victoria poets. He reads locally in Victoria and is completing his degree in Writing at University of Victoria.

JULIA MCCARTHY's poetry has been published widely in Canada and the U.S.

MARK MILNER lives and writes in Vancouver. He has published poetry and short fiction in a number of Canadian magazines and journals, including *Dandelion, Ariel, SancCrit,* and *WestWord.*

MIKE MULLEY is currently a student at SMUS in Victoria, B.C. He prefers dogs.

SHARON PAGE writes best late at night. She hopes to continue writing, though cell models are her real forte.

JENNIFER PATTERSON attends The Study, an independent school for girls in Westmount, Quebec. She has received recognition and awards for her acting and writing. She is also an avid snowboarder and the captain of the senior volleyball team.

ALISON PICK lives in Guelph where she won first place in The Bookshelf's first annual poetry contest. She received an honourable mention in the Cambridge Writers' Collective contest, and will appear in their anthology *Writers Under Cover.* She has been published in *The New Quarterly.*

RUTH ROACH PIERSON has taken early retirement from teaching women's history and feminist studies at the Ontario Institute for Studies in Education of the University of Toronto to devote herself full-time to poetry writing.

MARYELLEN POLIKOFF is a B.C. poet and a part-time investment representative. She is a graduate of New College of California in San Francisco in 1986.

SUZANNE ROBERTSON was born in Perth, Ontario. She is a renowned expert in many fields and has changed careers only three times in the past two years. She lives and writes in Toronto.

LAISHA ROSNAU is a writer who divides her time between Vancouver and elsewhere. Her work has appeared, or is forthcoming, in several journals, including *The Antigonish Review, Canadian Literature, Event,* and *The Malahat Review.* She is currently the Executive Director of *Prism international* and is completing an MFA at UBC.

EMILY ROSSER lives in Georgetown, Ontario. She is eighteen years old and is finishing her last year of high school. Writing is what keeps her going when things in life start to get out of control.

JAY RUZESKY's books include *Painting the Yellow House Blue* (Anansi, 1994) and *Writing on the Wall* (Outlaw Editions, 1996). This poem is from a new manuscript "Blue Himalayan Poppies." He lives in Victoria, B.C.

E. RUSSELL SMITH writes in Ottawa. His first volume of poetry *Why We Stand Facing South* was selected as one of the Literary Network's Top Ten Canadian Poetry Books for Fall 1999. His poetry has been published across Canada and in the U.K. and was chosen for *Vintage 95.*

LENORA STEELE has had poetry accepted or published in *Room of One's Own, The Windsor Review, The Fiddlehead, The New Quarterly,* and *The Antigonish Review,* among others.

SUSAN STENSON won first prize in the League's National Poetry Contest in 1999. Her first book will be published in fall 2000 by Sono Nis Press. She lives in Victoria.

In the two years PETER STUHLMANN has been writing he has had poems appear in *Zygote* and *Bywords*. He lives and writes in Ottawa.

RUSSELL THORNTON is a North Vancouver poet. His collection *The Fifth Window* was published in 2000 by Thistledown Press. In addition to his own poetry, he publishes his translations of the work of the classical Persian poet, Hafez.

EVA TIHANYI's fourth collection of poetry, *Restoring the Wickedness,* was published by Thistledown Press in 1999. She teaches full time at Niagara College in Welland, Ontario.

LEAH TODD loves to write, play music and participate in every fun aspect of life. She is thrilled to be awarded the privilege of publication!

MILDRED TREMBLAY lives in Nanaimo, B.C. She has published a book of short fiction, and her first book of poetry will be published by Oolichan later this year. In recent years she has won both the League's National Poetry Contest and the *Arc Magazine* Poetry Prize.

ALISON WATT is a writer and visual artist. Her poetry has appeared in *Backwater Review, Amethyst Review* and *Vintage 98.* She lives on Protection Island, near Nanaimo, B.C.

MARGO WHEATON lives in Halifax with her daughter Jennifer. Her poems have appeared in *The Fiddlehead, Pottersfield Portfolio, Room of One's Own* and *Contemporary Verse II.*

SUE WHEELER's first book *Solstice on the Anacortes Ferry* (Kalamalka Press, 1995) won the Kalamalka New Writers Award and was shortlisted for the Pat Lowther and the Gerald Lampert Memorial Awards. Her poems have won the Gwendolyn MacEwen Memorial Award and the *Malahat* Long Poem Prize. Her second collection, *Slow-Moving Target,* is from Brick Books.

PATRICIA YOUNG's most recent book is *Ruin and Beauty: New and Selected Poems* (Anansi, 2000). She lives in Victoria, B.C.

TERENCE YOUNG's first book of poetry, *The Island in Winter*, was published in 1999 by Véhicule Press, and was short listed for the 1999 Governor General's Poetry Award and for the Gerald Lampert Memorial Award. His first collection of stories will appear in fall 2000.

1988	1st poem:	Michael Redhill
	2nd poem:	Sharon Thesen
	3rd poem:	Cornelia Hoogland
1989	1st poem:	Elisabeth Harvor
	tied:	Elyse Yates St. George
	tied:	Patricia Young
1990	1st poem:	Diana Brebner
	2nd poem:	Blaine Marchand
	3rd poem:	D.J. Eastwood
1991	1st poem:	Elisabeth Harvor
	2nd poem:	David Margoshes
	3rd poem:	Debbie Fersht
1992	1st poem:	Nadine McInnis
	2nd poem:	Stan Rogal
	3rd poem:	Louise B. Halfe
1993	1st poem:	Joy Kirstin
	2nd poem:	Patricia Young
	3rd poem:	Gabrielle Guenther
1994	1st poem:	Tim Bowling
	2nd poem:	John Pass
	3rd poem:	Sue McLeod
1995	1st poem:	Catherine Greenwood
	2nd poem:	Sophia Kaszuba
	3rd poem:	Neile Graham
1996	1st poem:	Patricia Young
	2nd poem:	Mildred Tremblay
	3rd poem:	Rafi Aaron

1997   1st poem: Marlene Cookshaw
         2nd poem: Patricia Young
         3rd poem: Linda Rogers

1998   1st poem: Esta Spalding
         2nd poem: Deanna Yonge
             tied: Faizal Deen Forrester
             tied: Richard Lemm

1999   1st poem: Susan Stenson
         2nd poem: Peter Richardson
         3rd poem: Brent MacLaine